My Equestrian tr
Journal

This book belongs to:

_____

My name: _____

My Age: _____

My Instructor's name: _____

_____

Veterinarian's name: _____

_____

Love You

A special Request

"If you enjoy this book, could you please do me a favor?

Please take a moment to leave your review on Amazon review page for our books.

Please spare your time to write just a few words, it will help us alot!

thank you for your support.

For more,

Email: gkonekitio@gmail.com

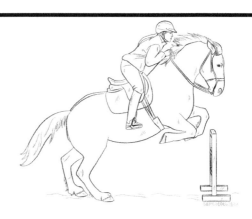

The horse, a gregarious animal:

The domestic behavior of the horse is inspired by the wild state where the animal lives in herd, a group of less than ten horses. The herd consists of a stallion, a few mares (usually three) and foals. When the young ones reach adulthood, they in turn leave to build up their herd. A domestic horse has a gregarious instinct, it prefers to be in a group.

Grooming the horse:

This activity is very important in the relationship with the horse. Through this care, we establish a complicity with him. Grooming does not simply consist of brushing the animal's coat but includes several gestures such as massage, cleaning and untangling. If it is partly to make him more beautiful, the fact of grooming a horse ensures him a better hygiene and has consequences on his health. It is an opportunity to tone his muscles by massaging them, but also to identify any injuries he may have. It is practiced daily.

The salt stone:

It is not uncommon for ruminants to have a salt stone, but it can be indispensable for horses as well. This large block is licked by the animal and constitutes a food supplement. It contains various mineral salts that are sometimes lacking in a diet based on hay, straw and oats. It brings the necessary trace elements to the horse, and helps it to recover after the effort. It can be hung in the meadow or placed in a specially designed feeder in the stall.

The white marks

Horse coats have spots that are specific in shape and position. Here are some names given to them:

the balzane is a kind of "sock" of white hair that begins just above the hoof;

the header is found on the horse's forehead and can be white hair markings of different shapes;

the "list" is the white band that marks the horse's muzzle

The halter:

The halter is a harness that is placed on the horse's head. It can be made of leather or nylon, but can also be improvised with a lead rope. If it is not absolutely essential when the horse is in pasture or in its box, the halter is useful in all other activities. It allows the rider to lead the horse when it is not mounted, or to tie it up when grooming. There are different shapes of halters: the most common ones have a classic harness shape, while those intended for presentation can r and more discreet.

Horse halter

The horseshoe:

Useful for correcting a horse's plumbness as well as for protecting the horn of its hooves, the horseshoe is applied by the farrier. It consists in applying a metal U on the part of the hoof that is in permanent contact with the ground. The shoe is made to measure, and prevents wear and tear when the horse makes long journeys. It is necessary to change the shoes very regularly because the horn sometimes grows faster than it wears.

Cold bloodedness:

Although there is no difference in temperature between the different horses, the expression hot-blooded or cold-blooded is used to characterize certain types of breeds. In reality, this differentiation is more about the origin of the breeds: hot-blooded horses are mostly from warm countries, while cold-blooded horses are mainly from northern Europe. In the first category, we find the Thoroughbreds, and in the second, the draught horses. Horses resulting from crossbreeding between these two types are called half-bloods.

Gait of the horse:

Unlike a human who walks or runs, the horse has several gaits that correspond to its speed of movement. They are called gaits. The walk is the slowest, it corresponds to our walk. Next comes the trot, which is a little faster and slightly hopped. The gallop, finally, is a very fast way of running. A well-trained horse can learn "choreographed" gaits from humans in addition to these three natural gaits.

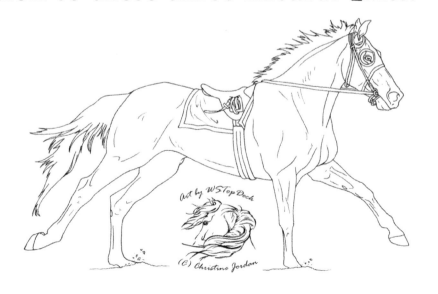

Horse or stallion?:

Depending on whether it is a male or a female, a breeder or a small horse, it has a distinctive name. The stallion, a name often abused to qualify all kinds of male horses, indicates in reality only the recognized reproducer. The mare gives birth to foals but also to their sisters, the fillies. As for the gelding, it is a castrated male. The pony is not a separate species but a small horse. Several breeds of horses are ponies because they are less than 1.48 m at the withers.

The bit:

The bit, a metal cylinder placed in the horse's mouth and connected to the reins, is used to lead the horse. How do you place it without hurting the horse? The horse's jaw is made up of two parts. At the front, a row of incisors at the top and bottom is used to catch grass and leaves, while at the back, the teeth are decorated with premolars and molars. Between these two types of teeth there is a space without teeth. This is where the bit is placed.

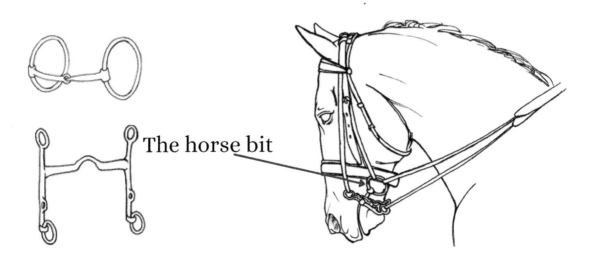

The horse bit

How to take care of your horse?

When you have a horse, riding is not the only thing to consider. In order for him to live in the best conditions, he must also be fed, groomed and cleaned. The point.

Feeding the horse:

The horse should be fed 3 times a day. Ideally, you should feed a combination of forage grasses and hay. You should also give him a measured amount of concentrate. Not forgetting the water that you must make available to him.

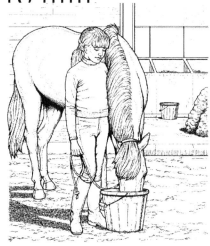

Cleaning the horse:

In principle, you should clean your horse every day. But if he is regularly outside, it is useless to clean him daily, at the risk of removing the natural oils which protect them from the bad weather.

Taking the horse out of the pasture:

An essential element not to forget every day: taking the horse out of the pasture. Only, you must make sure that they do not have any bites or scratches.

Clean your hooves with a foot cleaner:

Cleaning the hoof with a foot cleaner is important to protect it. Just be careful! Don't forget that the 'V' shape in his hoof is a very sensitive area. So, clean carefully and gently, because a wrong move can hurt your pet.

Shearing the horse:

If your horse works regularly, it should be clipped regularly so that it can be in the right condition at all times and dry quickly when it sweats.

It is also important to shear horses as soon as it gets cold. To make the task easier, opt for cordless clippers.

Brush its mane and tail with a comb:

When brushing the horse's tail with a comb, remember that you should be standing on the side, not directly on the back, otherwise you can make it expel. However, be careful, so as not to tear the tangles.

Mane and Tail Combs

Good to know:

After the training session, if the horse is sweaty, do not let him drink a lot of water, a few sips are enough. On the other hand, it is better to encourage him to take a few walks to cool down.

Fun Horse Facts for Kids:

Check out some fun horse facts for kids and enjoy learning a wide range of interesting information about horses. Find out the difference between a colt and a filly, read about horses funny sleeping habits, how fast they run and much more.

- *Horses can sleep both lying down and standing up.*

- *Horses can run shortly after birth.*

- *Domestic horses have a lifespan of around 25 years.*

- *A 19th century horse named 'Old Billy' is said to have lived 62 years.*

- *Horses have around 205 bones in their skeleton.*

- *Horses have been domesticated for over 5000 years.*

- *Horses are herbivores (plant eaters).*

- *Horses have bigger eyes than any other mammal that lives on land.*

- *Because horse's eyes are on the side of their head they are capable of seeing nearly 360 degrees at one time.*

- *Horses gallop at around 44 kph (27 mph).*

- *The fastest recorded sprinting speed of a horse was 88 kph (55 mph).*

- *Estimates suggest that there are around 60 million horses in the world.*

- *Scientists believe that horses have evolved over the past 50 million years from much smaller creatures.*

- *A male horse is called a stallion.*

- *A female horse is called a mare.*

- *A young male horse is called a colt.*

- *A young female horse is called a filly.*

- *Ponies are small horses.*

Fun Pony Facts for Kids:

Check out a range of fun pony facts for kids. Learn what they look like, what they are used for, what makes them unique and much more.

Read on and enjoy a variety of interesting information about ponies.

- **Ponies are small horses.**

- **Ponies have thicker manes and tails than horses.**

- *Well trained ponies are good for children while they are learning to ride.*

- *As well as for riding, ponies are used in driving and working roles.*

- *Young ponies are called foals.*

- *Shetland ponies are small but very strong.*

- *Pound for pound, ponies are stronger than horses.*

- *Miniature horses are even smaller than ponies*

- *Hackney ponies were first bred to pull carriages.*

- *Ponies are easy to look after, requiring half the food that a horse would if it was the same weight.*

Other Equestrian items:

Ear Net

Bridle

Saddle

Blanket

Saddle pod

Protection boots

Helmet

Equestrian boots

Lead and Hoof pick

What Should I Have in My Horse's First Aid Kit?

First Aid Basics Kit
- ✓ Thermometer
- ✓ Standing wraps or polo wraps
- ✓ Eye wash
- ✓ Hoof pick
- ✓ Halter/lead rope
- ✓ Flashlight/headlamp with batteries
- ✓ Pelleted complete feed such as Equine Senior or grass pellets
- ✓ Stethoscope (practice listening to horse's gut sounds at different times of day)
- ✓ Watch with second hand

Foot Abscess Kit
- ✓ Epsom salts
- ✓ Animalintex pad or Magnapaste
- ✓ Diaper (infant to size 2, depending on size of horse)
- ✓ Vet wrap

Laceration Kit
- ✓ Permanent marker
- ✓ Gloves
- ✓ Nolvasan/Betadine solution
- ✓ Gauze squares
- ✓ Superglue
- ✓ Triple antibiotic ointment
- ✓ Non-adhesive pads (Telfa is a typical brand found at feed stores)
- ✓ Cotton sheet/combine leg wrap
- ✓ Gauze roll
- ✓ Vet wrap
- ✓ Bandage scissors

From Your Veterinarian
- ✓ Banamine
- ✓ Bute

Other
- ✓ _____
- ✓ _____
- ✓ _____
- ✓ _____
- ✓ _____
- ✓ _____

11308 92nd St SE, Snohomish

Trail Rider Checklist

Your Where to Ride Guide

In the Truck / Trailer

- [ ] Road Map and Directions to trailhead
- [ ] Registration / Insurance
- [ ] Coggins Papers / Health Papers
- [ ] Flashlight w/ spare batteries
- [ ] Spare Tire Truck / Trailer
- [ ] Jack & Lug Wrench - Truck and Trailer
- [ ] Chock Blocks for Wheels
- [ ] Manure Rake / Forks
- [ ] Manure bucket
- [ ] Spares
  - Extra Cinch / Girth
  - Headstall / Bridle
  - Reins
  - Halter and Lead
- [ ] Tools – Pliers / Screwdriver
- [ ] Duct tape
- [ ] Garbage bags

_____

_____

Tack

- [ ] Saddle
- [ ] Bridle
- [ ] Saddle Pads
- [ ] Saddle / Pommel Bags
- [ ] Halter
- [ ] Hobbles
- [ ] Breast Collar
- [ ] Crupper / Breechin
- [ ] Cinch / Girth

_____

_____

Equine Supplies

- [ ] Feed – Hay / Grain
- [ ] Feed and Water Buckets
- [ ] Water
- [ ] Hay Bag
- [ ] Horse First Aid Kit
- [ ] Fly Spray
- [ ] Hoof Pick
- [ ] Sponge or rag
- [ ] Grooming Supplies

_____

_____

Personal Supplies

- [ ] Riding Pants and Jeans
- [ ] Riding Boots
- [ ] Socks
- [ ] Outerwear Jacket / Sweater
- [ ] Rain Gear
- [ ] Undergarments
- [ ] Extra Set of Keys
- [ ] Knife
- [ ] Lip Balm
- [ ] Hat - Gloves
- [ ] Helmet
- [ ] Sun Block
- [ ] Insect Repellent
- [ ] First Aid Kit
- [ ] Toilet Paper / Wet Ones
- [ ] Medications

_____

_____

_____

_____

_____

_____

On the Trail

- [ ] Hoof Pick
- [ ] Knife / Wire Cutters
- [ ] Map of the Trail / Compass
- [ ] Water Bottle
- [ ] Snacks
- [ ] Saddle Bag / Pommel Bags
- [ ] Helmet
- [ ] Insect Repellent
- [ ] First Aid Kit
- [ ] Rain Slicker
- [ ] Cell Phone/Way to call for help
- [ ] Rope/ cord for repairs
- [ ] Lead rope
- [ ] Sun Block
- [ ] Camera
- [ ] Lighter

_____

_____

Camp Equipment

- [ ] Tent / Hammock
- [ ] Sleeping bag
- [ ] Camp Shoes/Mud Boots
- [ ] Lantern
- [ ] Food
- [ ] Camp Stove
- [ ] Air mattress
- [ ] Flashlight
- [ ] First Aid Kit
- [ ] Insect Repellent
- [ ] Camp Chairs
- [ ] Folding table
- [ ] Highline gear

_____

_____

HORSE INFORMATION RECORD

HORSE NAME _____

BARN NAME —————————— BREED ——————

DATE OF BIRTH _____ SEX _____

COLOR _____ HEIGHT _____

REGISTRATION # _____ TATTOO _____

WHERE STABLED _____

PHONE NUMBER _____ *EMAIL* _____

VETERINARIAN _____

PHONE NUMBER _____ *EMAIL* _____

FARRIER _____

PHONE NUMBER _____ *EMAIL* _____

TRAINER _____

PHONE NUMBER _____ *EMAIL* _____

Breed_____

The Basick

_____
_____
_____
_____
_____

Intresting facts about this breed

_____
_____
_____
_____
_____
_____
_____

Draw a picture of the breed

Riding Lesson Journal

Date_____

_____

_____

Describe your Lesson:_____

_____

_____

Name 3 things that you learned today

1._____

_____

2._____

_____

3._____

_____

Need to improve

☐ ——————
——————
☐ ——————
——————
☐ ——————
——————
☐ ——————
——————
☐ ——————
——————
☐ ——————
——————
☐ ——————
——————
☐ ——————
——————
☐ ——————
——————

"You can do it!"

Name something you didn't understand during your lesson today.

_____

_____

What can you do to figure it out?

_____

_____

HORSE INFORMATION RECORD

HORSE NAME _____

BARN NAME————————————BREED _____

DATE OF BIRTH _____ SEX _____

COLOR _____ HEIGHT _____

REGISTRATION # _____ TATTOO _____

WHERE STABLED _____

PHONE NUMBER _____ *EMAIL* _____

VETERINARIAN _____

PHONE NUMBER _____ *EMAIL* _____

FARRIER _____

PHONE NUMBER _____ *EMAIL* _____

TRAINER _____

PHONE NUMBER _____ *EMAIL* _____

Breed_____

The Basick

_____
_____
_____
_____
_____

Intresting facts about this breed

_____
_____
_____
_____
_____
_____
_____

Draw a picture of the breed

Riding Lesson Journal

Date_____

☐ _____

☐ _____

☐ _____

☐ _____

☐ _____

☐ _____

☐ _____

☐ _____

☐ _____

☐ _____

_____

_____

Describe your Lesson:_____

_____

_____

Name 3 things that you learned today

1._____

_____

2. _____

_____

3. _____

_____

"You can do it!"

Name something you didn't understand during your lesson today.

_____

_____

What can you do to figure it out?

_____

_____

HORSE INFORMATION RECORD

HORSE NAME _____

BARN NAME —————————— BREED _____

DATE OF BIRTH _____ SEX _____

COLOR _____ HEIGHT_____

REGISTRATION # _____ TATTOO _____

WHERE STABLED _____

PHONE NUMBER _____ *EMAIL* _____

VETERINARIAN _____

PHONE NUMBER _____ *EMAIL* _____

FARRIER _____

PHONE NUMBER _____ *EMAIL* _____

TRAINER _____

PHONE NUMBER _____ *EMAIL* _____

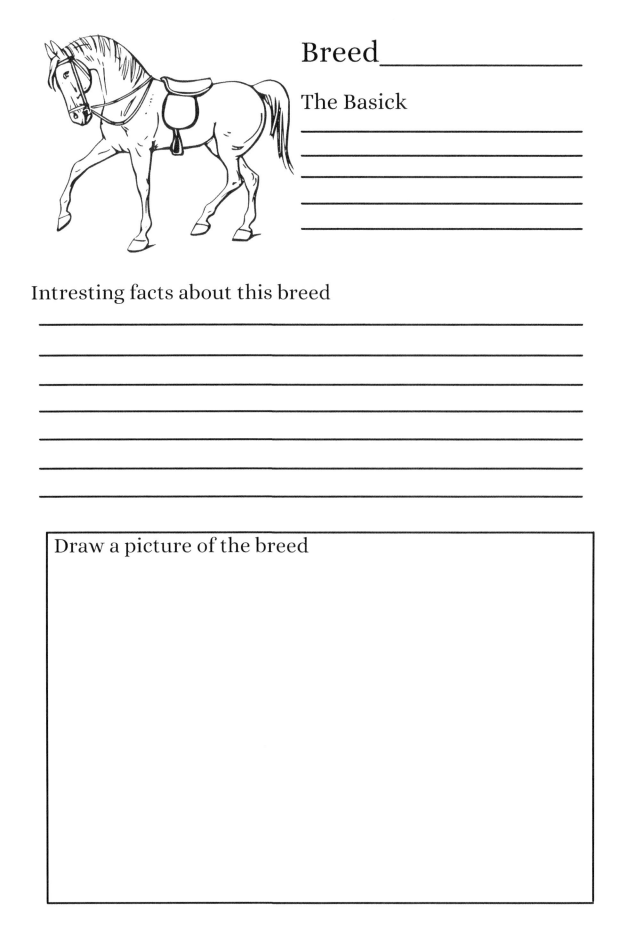

Breed_____

The Basick

_____
_____
_____
_____
_____

Intresting facts about this breed

_____
_____
_____
_____
_____
_____
_____

Draw a picture of the breed

Riding Lesson Journal

Date_____

_____

_____

Describe your Lesson:_____

_____

_____

Name 3 things that you learned today

1._____

_____

2. _____

_____

3. _____

_____

Name something you didn't understand during your lesson today.

_____

_____

What can you do to figure it out?

_____

_____

HORSE INFORMATION RECORD

HORSE NAME _____

BARN NAME————————————BREED _____

DATE OF BIRTH _____SEX _____

COLOR _____ HEIGHT_____

REGISTRATION # _____TATTOO _____

WHERE STABLED _____

PHONE NUMBER _____ *EMAIL* _____

VETERINARIAN_____

PHONE NUMBER _____ *EMAIL* _____

FARRIER_____

PHONE NUMBER _____ *EMAIL* _____

TRAINER_____

PHONE NUMBER _____ *EMAIL* _____

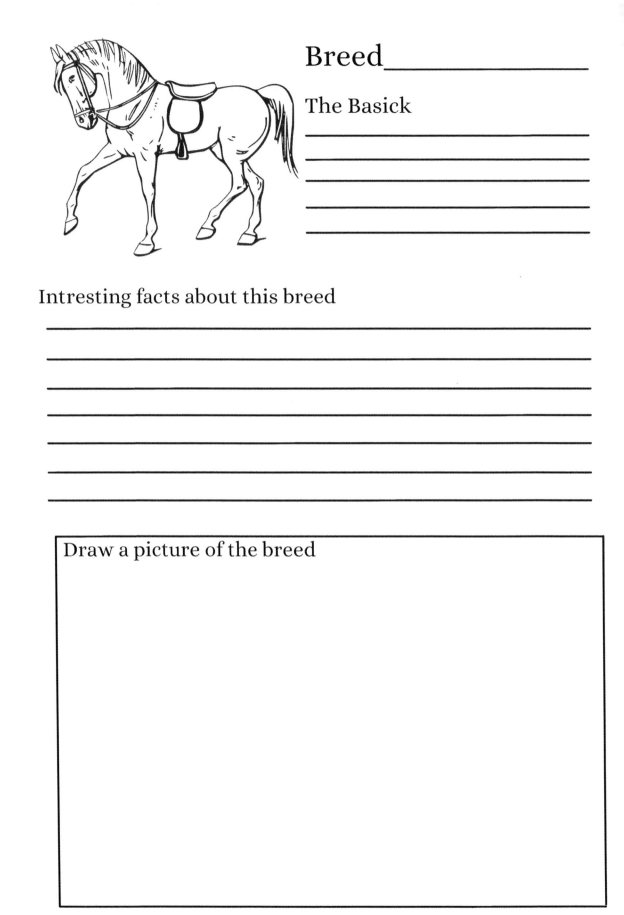

Breed_____

The Basick

_____
_____
_____
_____
_____

Intresting facts about this breed

_____
_____
_____
_____
_____
_____
_____

Draw a picture of the breed

Riding Lesson Journal

Date_____

_____

_____

Describe your Lesson:_____

_____

_____

Name 3 things that you learned today

1._____

_____

2._____

_____

3._____

_____

Need to improve

☐ _____
☐ _____
☐ _____
☐ _____
☐ _____
☐ _____
☐ _____
☐ _____
☐ _____
☐ _____

"You can do it!"

Name something you didn't understand during your lesson today.

_____

_____

What can you do to figure it out?

_____

_____

HORSE INFORMATION RECORD

HORSE NAME _____

BARN NAME ———————————— BREED _____

DATE OF BIRTH _____ SEX _____

COLOR _____ HEIGHT _____

REGISTRATION # _____ TATTOO _____

WHERE STABLED _____

PHONE NUMBER _____ *EMAIL* _____

VETERINARIAN _____

PHONE NUMBER _____ *EMAIL* _____

FARRIER _____

PHONE NUMBER _____ *EMAIL* _____

TRAINER _____

PHONE NUMBER _____ *EMAIL* _____

Breed_____

The Basick

_____
_____
_____
_____
_____

Intresting facts about this breed

_____
_____
_____
_____
_____
_____
_____

Draw a picture of the breed

Riding Lesson Journal

Date_____

_____

_____

Describe your Lesson:_____

_____

_____

Name 3 things that you learned today

1._____

_____

2. _____

_____

3. _____

_____

Name something you didn't understand during your lesson today.

_____

_____

What can you do to figure it out?

_____

_____

Need to improve

☐ _____
_____

☐ _____
_____

☐ _____
_____

☐ _____
_____

☐ _____
_____

☐ _____
_____

☐ _____
_____

☐ _____
_____

☐ _____
_____

☐ _____

"You can do it!"

HORSE INFORMATION RECORD

HORSE NAME _____

BARN NAME _____ BREED _____

DATE OF BIRTH _____ SEX _____

COLOR _____ HEIGHT _____

REGISTRATION # _____ TATTOO _____

WHERE STABLED _____

PHONE NUMBER _____ *EMAIL* _____

VETERINARIAN _____

PHONE NUMBER _____ *EMAIL* _____

FARRIER _____

PHONE NUMBER _____ *EMAIL* _____

TRAINER _____

PHONE NUMBER _____ *EMAIL* _____

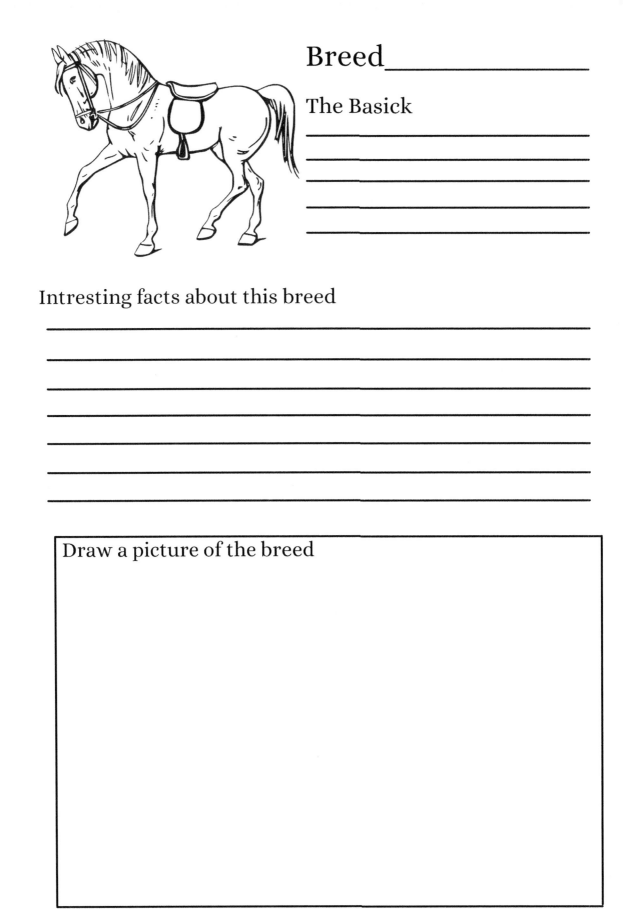

Breed_____

The Basick

_____
_____
_____
_____
_____

Intresting facts about this breed

_____
_____
_____
_____
_____
_____
_____

Draw a picture of the breed

Riding Lesson Journal

Date_____

_____

_____

Describe your Lesson:_____

_____

_____

Name 3 things that you learned today

1._____

_____

2. _____

_____

3. _____

_____

Name something you didn't understand during your lesson today.

_____

_____

What can you do to figure it out?

_____

_____

HORSE INFORMATION RECORD

HORSE NAME _____

BARN NAME ———————————— BREED _____

DATE OF BIRTH _____ SEX _____

COLOR _____ HEIGHT_____

REGISTRATION # _____ TATTOO _____

WHERE STABLED _____

PHONE NUMBER _____ *EMAIL* _____

VETERINARIAN_____

PHONE NUMBER _____ *EMAIL* _____

FARRIER_____

PHONE NUMBER _____ *EMAIL* _____

TRAINER_____

PHONE NUMBER _____ *EMAIL* _____

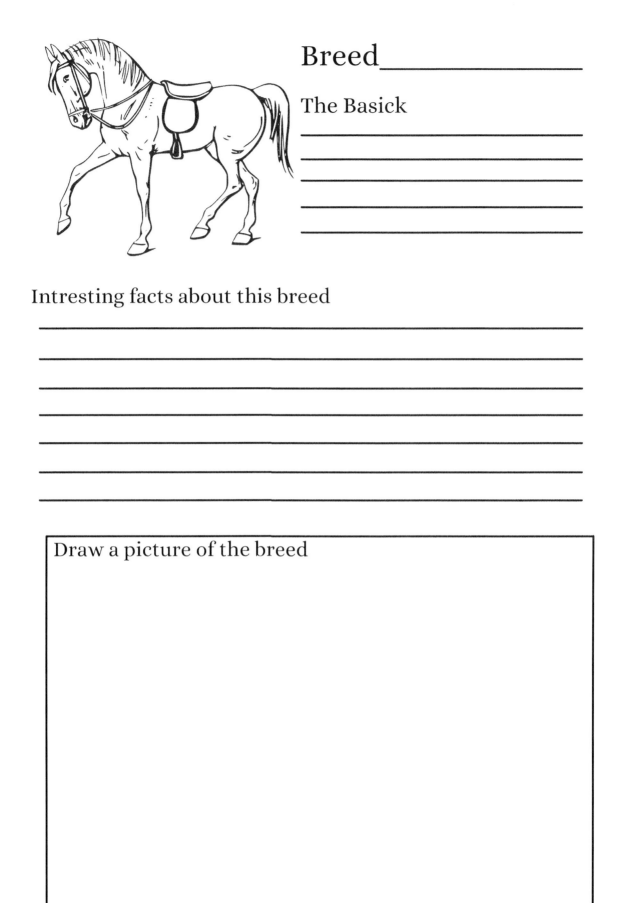

Breed_____

The Basick

_____
_____
_____
_____
_____

Intresting facts about this breed

_____
_____
_____
_____
_____
_____
_____

Draw a picture of the breed

Riding Lesson Journal

Date_____

_____

_____

Describe your Lesson:_____

_____

_____

Name 3 things that you learned today

1._____

_____

2. _____

_____

3. _____

_____

Name something you didn't understand during your lesson today.

_____

_____

What can you do to figure it out?

_____

_____

HORSE INFORMATION RECORD

HORSE NAME _____

BARN NAME ————————————— BREED _____

DATE OF BIRTH _____ SEX _____

COLOR _____ HEIGHT _____

REGISTRATION # _____ TATTOO _____

WHERE STABLED _____

PHONE NUMBER _____ *EMAIL* _____

VETERINARIAN _____

PHONE NUMBER _____ *EMAIL* _____

FARRIER _____

PHONE NUMBER _____ *EMAIL* _____

TRAINER _____

PHONE NUMBER _____ *EMAIL* _____

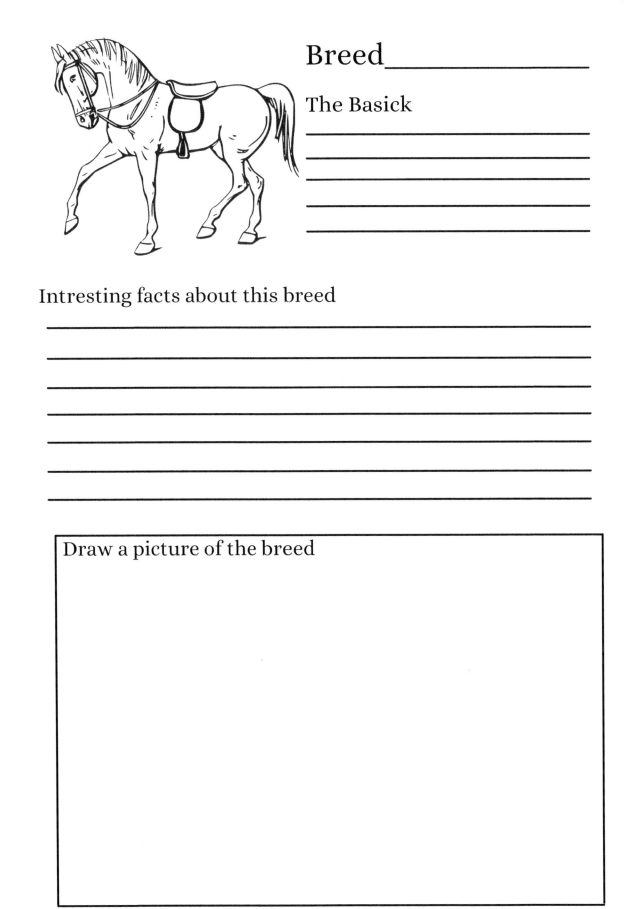

Breed_____

The Basick

_____
_____
_____
_____
_____

Intresting facts about this breed

_____
_____
_____
_____
_____
_____
_____

Draw a picture of the breed

Riding Lesson Journal

Date_____

_____

_____

Describe your Lesson:_____

_____

_____

Name 3 things that you learned today

1._____

_____

2._____

_____

3._____

_____

Need to improve

☐ ————
☐ ————
☐ ————
☐ ————
☐ ————
☐ ————
☐ ————
☐ ————
☐ ————
☐ ————

"You can do it!"

Name something you didn't understand during your lesson today.

_____

_____

What can you do to figure it out?

_____

_____

HORSE INFORMATION RECORD

HORSE NAME _____

BARN NAME ——————————— BREED _____

DATE OF BIRTH _____ SEX _____

COLOR _____ HEIGHT _____

REGISTRATION # _____ TATTOO _____

WHERE STABLED _____

PHONE NUMBER _____ *EMAIL* _____

VETERINARIAN _____

PHONE NUMBER _____ *EMAIL* _____

FARRIER _____

PHONE NUMBER _____ *EMAIL* _____

TRAINER _____

PHONE NUMBER _____ *EMAIL* _____

Breed_____

The Basick

_____
_____
_____
_____
_____

Intresting facts about this breed

_____
_____
_____
_____
_____
_____
_____

Draw a picture of the breed

Riding Lesson Journal

Date_____

_____

_____

Describe your Lesson:_____

_____

_____

Name 3 things that you learned today

1._____

_____

2. _____

_____

3. _____

_____

Name something you didn't understand during your lesson today.

_____

_____

What can you do to figure it out?

_____

_____

Need to improve

☐ _____
_____

☐ _____
_____

☐ _____
_____

☐ _____
_____

☐ _____
_____

☐ _____
_____

☐ _____
_____

☐ _____
_____

☐ _____
_____

☐ _____
_____

"You can do it!"

HORSE INFORMATION RECORD

HORSE NAME _____

BARN NAME——————————BREED _____

DATE OF BIRTH_____SEX _____

COLOR _____ HEIGHT_____

REGISTRATION # _____TATTOO _____

WHERE STABLED _____

PHONE NUMBER _____ *EMAIL* _____

VETERINARIAN_____

PHONE NUMBER _____ *EMAIL* _____

FARRIER_____

PHONE NUMBER _____ *EMAIL* _____

TRAINER_____

PHONE NUMBER _____ *EMAIL* _____

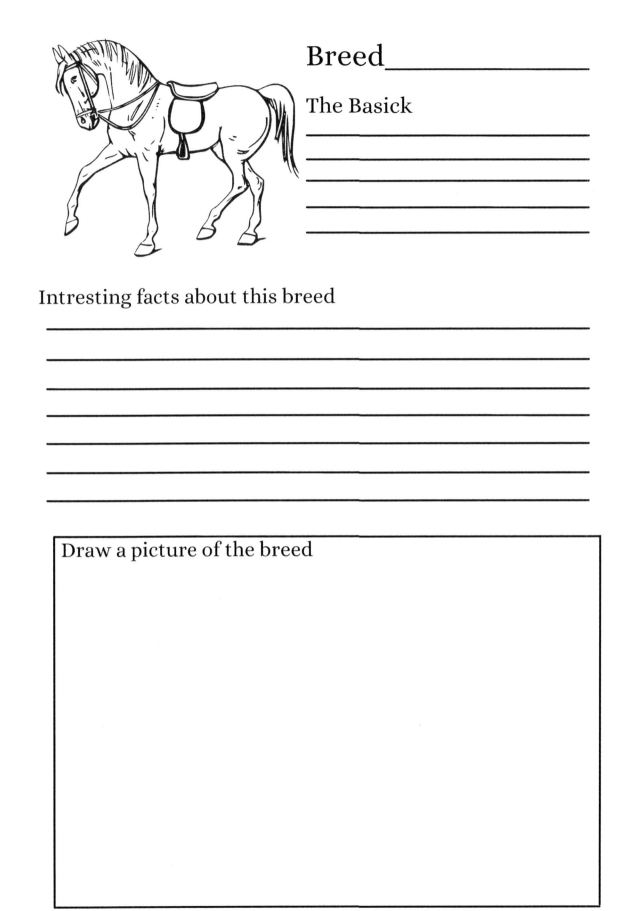

Breed_____

The Basick

_____
_____
_____
_____
_____

Intresting facts about this breed

_____
_____
_____
_____
_____
_____
_____

Draw a picture of the breed

Riding Lesson Journal

Date_____

_____

_____

Describe your Lesson:_____

_____

_____

Name 3 things that you learned today

1._____

_____

2. _____

_____

3. _____

_____

Name something you didn't understand during your lesson today.

_____

_____

What can you do to figure it out?

_____

_____

HORSE INFORMATION RECORD

HORSE NAME _____

BARN NAME————————————BREED _____

DATE OF BIRTH_____SEX _____

COLOR _____ HEIGHT_____

REGISTRATION # _____TATTOO _____

WHERE STABLED _____

PHONE NUMBER _____ *EMAIL* _____

VETERINARIAN_____

PHONE NUMBER _____ *EMAIL* _____

FARRIER_____

*PHONE NUMBER*_____ *EMAIL* _____

TRAINER_____

PHONE NUMBER _____ *EMAIL* _____

Breed_____

The Basick

_____
_____
_____
_____
_____

Intresting facts about this breed

_____
_____
_____
_____
_____
_____
_____

Draw a picture of the breed

Riding Lesson Journal

Date_____

_____

_____

Describe your Lesson:_____

_____

_____

Name 3 things that you learned today

1._____

_____

2. _____

_____

3. _____

_____

Need to improve

☐ _____
☐ _____
☐ _____
☐ _____
☐ _____
☐ _____
☐ _____
☐ _____
☐ _____
☐ _____

"You can do it!"

Name something you didn't understand during your lesson today.

_____

_____

What can you do to figure it out?

_____

_____

HORSE INFORMATION RECORD

HORSE NAME _____

BARN NAME _____ BREED _____

DATE OF BIRTH _____ SEX _____

COLOR _____ HEIGHT_____

REGISTRATION # _____ TATTOO _____

WHERE STABLED _____

PHONE NUMBER _____ *EMAIL* _____

VETERINARIAN _____

PHONE NUMBER _____ *EMAIL* _____

FARRIER _____

PHONE NUMBER _____ *EMAIL* _____

TRAINER _____

PHONE NUMBER _____ *EMAIL* _____

Breed_____

The Basick

_____

_____

_____

_____

_____

Intresting facts about this breed

_____

_____

_____

_____

_____

_____

Draw a picture of the breed

Riding Lesson Journal

Date_____

Need to improve

☐ ——————
☐ ——————
☐ ——————
☐ ——————
☐ ——————
☐ ——————
☐ ——————
☐ ——————
☐ ——————
☐ ——————

Describe your Lesson:_____

Name 3 things that you learned today

1._____

2._____

3._____

"You can do it!"

Name something you didn't understand during your lesson today.

What can you do to figure it out?

HORSE INFORMATION RECORD

HORSE NAME _____

BARN NAME ————————————BREED _____

DATE OF BIRTH _____ SEX _____

COLOR _____ HEIGHT _____

REGISTRATION # _____ TATTOO _____

WHERE STABLED _____

PHONE NUMBER _____ *EMAIL* _____

VETERINARIAN _____

PHONE NUMBER _____ *EMAIL* _____

FARRIER _____

PHONE NUMBER _____ *EMAIL* _____

TRAINER _____

PHONE NUMBER _____ *EMAIL* _____

Breed_____

The Basick

_____
_____
_____
_____
_____

Intresting facts about this breed

_____
_____
_____
_____
_____
_____
_____

Draw a picture of the breed

Riding Lesson Journal

Date_____

_____

_____

Describe your Lesson:_____

_____

_____

Name 3 things that you learned today

1._____

_____

2._____

_____

3._____

_____

Name something you didn't understand during your lesson today.

_____

_____

What can you do to figure it out?

_____

_____

HORSE INFORMATION RECORD

HORSE NAME _____

BARN NAME———————————BREED _____

DATE OF BIRTH _____ SEX _____

COLOR _____ HEIGHT_____

REGISTRATION # _____ TATTOO _____

WHERE STABLED _____

PHONE NUMBER _____ *EMAIL* _____

VETERINARIAN _____

PHONE NUMBER _____ *EMAIL* _____

FARRIER _____

PHONE NUMBER _____ *EMAIL* _____

TRAINER _____

PHONE NUMBER _____ *EMAIL* _____

Breed_____

The Basick

_____
_____
_____
_____
_____

Intresting facts about this breed

_____
_____
_____
_____
_____
_____
_____

Draw a picture of the breed

Riding Lesson Journal

Date_____

_____

_____

Describe your Lesson:_____

_____

_____

Name 3 things that you learned today

1._____

_____

2. _____

_____

3. _____

_____

Name something you didn't understand during your lesson today.

_____

_____

What can you do to figure it out?

_____

_____

Need to improve

☐ _____
☐ _____
☐ _____
☐ _____
☐ _____
☐ _____
☐ _____
☐ _____
☐ _____
☐ _____

"You can do it!"

HORSE INFORMATION RECORD

HORSE NAME _____

BARN NAME——————————BREED _____

DATE OF BIRTH_____SEX _____

COLOR _____ HEIGHT_____

REGISTRATION # _____TATTOO _____

WHERE STABLED _____

PHONE NUMBER _____ *EMAIL* _____

VETERINARIAN_____

PHONE NUMBER _____ *EMAIL* _____

FARRIER_____

PHONE NUMBER _____ *EMAIL* _____

TRAINER_____

PHONE NUMBER _____ *EMAIL* _____

Breed_____

The Basick

_____
_____
_____
_____
_____

Intresting facts about this breed

_____
_____
_____
_____
_____
_____
_____

Draw a picture of the breed

Riding Lesson Journal

Date_____

_____

_____

Describe your Lesson:_____

_____

_____

Name 3 things that you learned today

1._____

_____

2. _____

_____

3. _____

_____

Need to improve

- ☐ _____
- ☐ _____
- ☐ _____
- ☐ _____
- ☐ _____
- ☐ _____
- ☐ _____
- ☐ _____
- ☐ _____
- ☐ _____

"You can do it!"

Name something you didn't understand during your lesson today.

_____

_____

What can you do to figure it out?

_____

_____

HORSE INFORMATION RECORD

HORSE NAME _____

BARN NAME ———————————— BREED _____

DATE OF BIRTH _____ SEX _____

COLOR _____ HEIGHT _____

REGISTRATION # _____ TATTOO _____

WHERE STABLED _____

PHONE NUMBER _____ *EMAIL* _____

VETERINARIAN _____

PHONE NUMBER _____ *EMAIL* _____

FARRIER _____

PHONE NUMBER _____ *EMAIL* _____

TRAINER _____

PHONE NUMBER _____ *EMAIL* _____

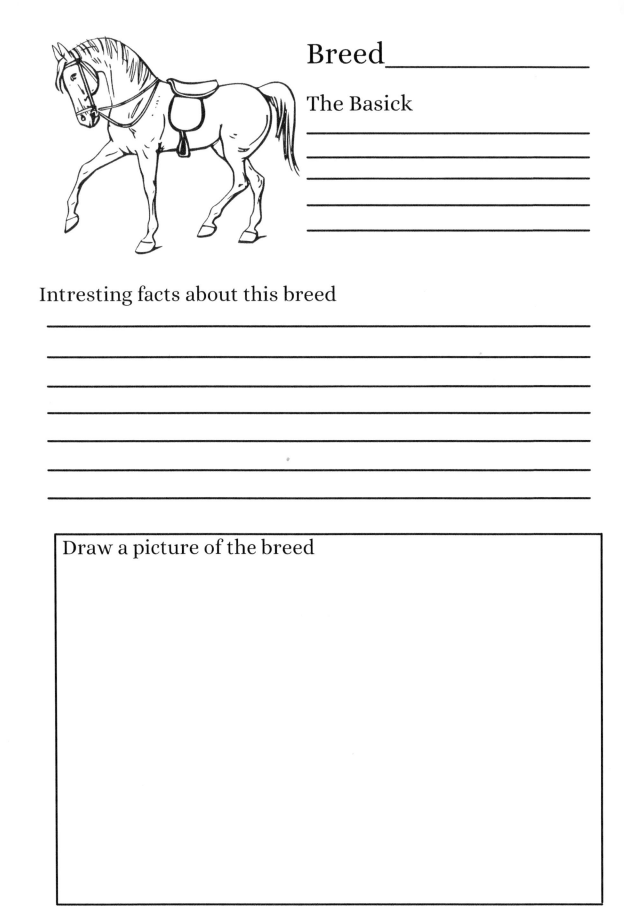

Breed_____

The Basick

_____
_____
_____
_____
_____

Intresting facts about this breed

_____
_____
_____
_____
_____
_____
_____

Draw a picture of the breed

Riding Lesson Journal

Date_____

_____

_____

Describe your Lesson:_____

_____

Name 3 things that you learned today

1._____

_____

2._____

_____

3._____

_____

Need to improve

☐ _____
☐ _____
☐ _____
☐ _____
☐ _____
☐ _____
☐ _____
☐ _____
☐ _____
☐ _____

"You can do it!"

Name something you didn't understand during your lesson today.

_____

_____

What can you do to figure it out?

_____

_____

HORSE INFORMATION RECORD

HORSE NAME _____

BARN NAME———————————BREED _____

DATE OF BIRTH_____SEX _____

COLOR _____ HEIGHT_____

REGISTRATION # _____TATTOO _____

WHERE STABLED _____

PHONE NUMBER _____ *EMAIL* _____

VETERINARIAN_____

PHONE NUMBER _____ *EMAIL* _____

FARRIER_____

PHONE NUMBER _____ *EMAIL* _____

TRAINER_____

PHONE NUMBER _____ *EMAIL* _____

Breed_____

The Basick

_____
_____
_____
_____
_____

Intresting facts about this breed

_____
_____
_____
_____
_____
_____
_____

Draw a picture of the breed

Riding Lesson Journal

Date_____

☐ ———————
☐ ———————
☐ ———————
☐ ———————
☐ ———————
☐ ———————
☐ ———————
☐ ———————
☐ ———————
☐ ———————

_____

_____

Describe your Lesson:_____

_____

_____

Name 3 things that you learned today

1._____

_____

2._____

_____

3._____

_____

"You can do it!"

Name something you didn't understand during your lesson today.

_____

_____

What can you do to figure it out?

_____

_____

HORSE INFORMATION RECORD

HORSE NAME _____

BARN NAME _____ BREED _____

DATE OF BIRTH _____ SEX _____

COLOR _____ HEIGHT _____

REGISTRATION # _____ TATTOO _____

WHERE STABLED _____

PHONE NUMBER _____ *EMAIL* _____

VETERINARIAN _____

PHONE NUMBER _____ *EMAIL* _____

FARRIER _____

PHONE NUMBER _____ *EMAIL* _____

TRAINER _____

PHONE NUMBER _____ *EMAIL* _____

Breed_____

The Basick

_____
_____
_____
_____
_____

Intresting facts about this breed

_____
_____
_____
_____
_____
_____
_____

Draw a picture of the breed

Riding Lesson Journal

Date _____

_____

_____

Describe your Lesson: _____

_____

_____

Name 3 things that you learned today

1. _____

_____

2. _____

_____

3. _____

_____

"You can do it!"

Name something you didn't understand during your lesson today.

_____

_____

What can you do to figure it out?

_____

_____

HORSE INFORMATION RECORD

HORSE NAME _____

BARN NAME——————————BREED _____

DATE OF BIRTH_____SEX _____

COLOR _____ HEIGHT_____

REGISTRATION # _____TATTOO _____

WHERE STABLED _____

PHONE NUMBER _____ *EMAIL* _____

VETERINARIAN_____

PHONE NUMBER _____ *EMAIL* _____

FARRIER_____

PHONE NUMBER _____ *EMAIL* _____

TRAINER_____

PHONE NUMBER _____ *EMAIL* _____

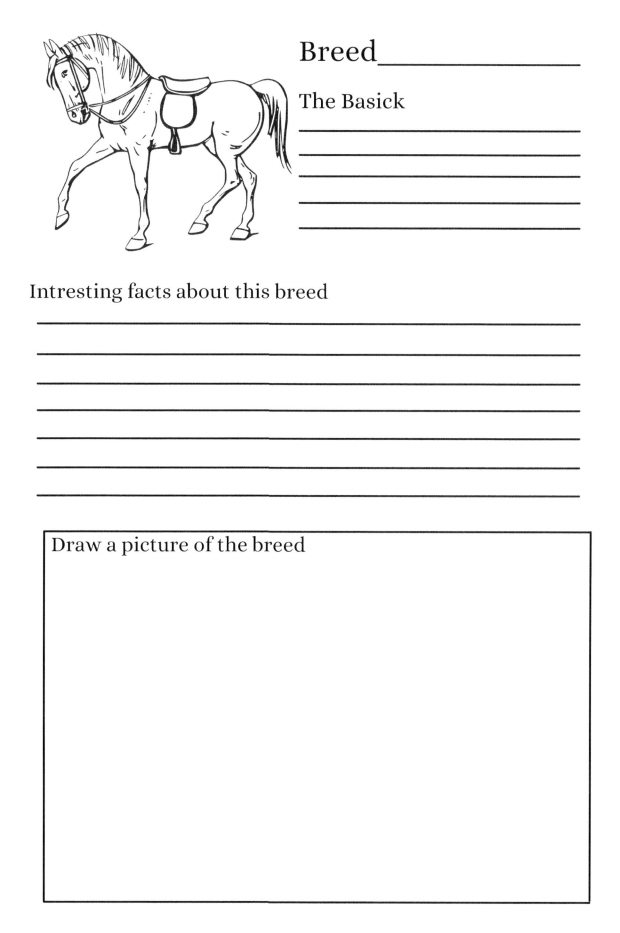

Breed_____

The Basick

_____
_____
_____
_____
_____

Intresting facts about this breed

_____
_____
_____
_____
_____
_____
_____

Draw a picture of the breed

Riding Lesson Journal

Date_____

_____

_____

Describe your Lesson:_____

_____

_____

Name 3 things that you learned today

1._____

_____

2._____

_____

3._____

"You can do it!"

_____

Name something you didn't understand during your lesson today.

_____

_____

What can you do to figure it out?

_____

_____

HORSE INFORMATION RECORD

HORSE NAME _____

BARN NAME ———————————— BREED _____

DATE OF BIRTH _____ SEX _____

COLOR _____ HEIGHT _____

REGISTRATION # _____ TATTOO _____

WHERE STABLED _____

PHONE NUMBER _____ *EMAIL* _____

VETERINARIAN _____

PHONE NUMBER _____ *EMAIL* _____

FARRIER _____

PHONE NUMBER _____ *EMAIL* _____

TRAINER _____

PHONE NUMBER _____ *EMAIL* _____

Breed_____

The Basick

_____
_____
_____
_____
_____

Intresting facts about this breed

_____
_____
_____
_____
_____
_____
_____

Draw a picture of the breed

Riding Lesson Journal

Date_____

_____

_____

Describe your Lesson:_____

_____

_____

Name 3 things that you learned today

1._____

_____

2. _____

_____

3. _____

_____

Need to improve

☐ _____
_____
☐ _____
_____
☐ _____
_____
☐ _____
_____
☐ _____
_____
☐ _____
_____
☐ _____
_____
☐ _____
_____
☐ _____
_____
☐ _____
_____

"You can do it!"

Name something you didn't understand during your lesson today.

_____

_____

What can you do to figure it out?

_____

_____

HORSE INFORMATION RECORD

HORSE NAME _____

BARN NAME _____ BREED _____

DATE OF BIRTH _____ SEX _____

COLOR _____ HEIGHT _____

REGISTRATION # _____ TATTOO _____

WHERE STABLED _____

PHONE NUMBER _____ *EMAIL* _____

VETERINARIAN _____

PHONE NUMBER _____ *EMAIL* _____

FARRIER _____

PHONE NUMBER _____ *EMAIL* _____

TRAINER _____

PHONE NUMBER _____ *EMAIL* _____

Breed_____

The Basick

_____
_____
_____
_____
_____

Intresting facts about this breed

_____
_____
_____
_____
_____
_____
_____
_____

Draw a picture of the breed

Riding Lesson Journal

Date_____

_____

_____

Describe your Lesson:_____

_____

_____

Name 3 things that you learned today

1._____

_____

2._____

_____

3._____

_____

Need to improve

☐ _____
_____
☐ _____
_____
☐ _____
_____
☐ _____
_____
☐ _____
_____
☐ _____
_____
☐ _____
_____
☐ _____
_____
☐ _____
_____
☐ _____
_____

"You can do it!"

Name something you didn't understand during your lesson today.

_____

_____

What can you do to figure it out?

_____

_____

HORSE INFORMATION RECORD

HORSE NAME _____

BARN NAME ————————— BREED _____

DATE OF BIRTH _____ SEX _____

COLOR _____ HEIGHT _____

REGISTRATION # _____ TATTOO _____

WHERE STABLED _____

PHONE NUMBER _____ *EMAIL* _____

VETERINARIAN _____

PHONE NUMBER _____ *EMAIL* _____

FARRIER _____

PHONE NUMBER _____ *EMAIL* _____

TRAINER _____

PHONE NUMBER _____ *EMAIL* _____

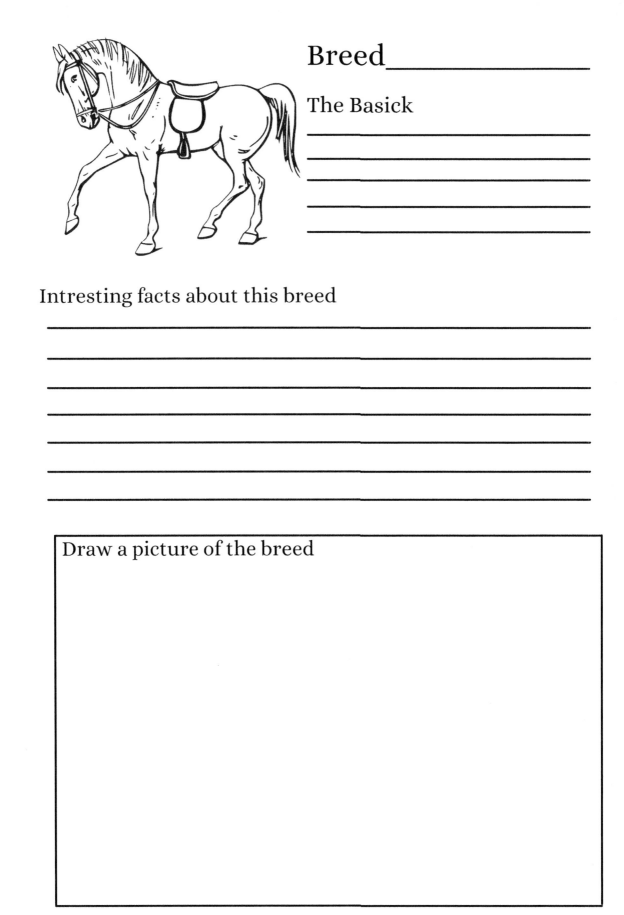

Breed_____

The Basick

_____
_____
_____
_____
_____

Intresting facts about this breed

_____
_____
_____
_____
_____
_____
_____

Draw a picture of the breed

Riding Lesson Journal

Date_____

_____

_____

Describe your Lesson:_____

_____

_____

Name 3 things that you learned today

1._____

_____

2. _____

_____

3. _____

_____

Name something you didn't understand during your lesson today.

_____

_____

What can you do to figure it out?

_____

_____

HORSE INFORMATION RECORD

HORSE NAME _____

BARN NAME —————————— BREED ———————

DATE OF BIRTH _____ SEX _____

COLOR _____ HEIGHT _____

REGISTRATION # _____ TATTOO _____

WHERE STABLED _____

PHONE NUMBER _____ *EMAIL* _____

VETERINARIAN _____

PHONE NUMBER _____ *EMAIL* _____

FARRIER _____

PHONE NUMBER _____ *EMAIL* _____

TRAINER _____

PHONE NUMBER _____ *EMAIL* _____

Breed_____

The Basick

_____
_____
_____
_____
_____

Intresting facts about this breed

_____
_____
_____
_____
_____
_____
_____

Draw a picture of the breed

Riding Lesson Journal

Date_____

_____

_____

Describe your Lesson:_____

_____

_____

Name 3 things that you learned today

1._____

_____

2._____

_____

3._____

_____

Need to improve

☐ _____
☐ _____
_____
☐ _____
☐ _____
☐ _____
☐ _____
_____
☐ _____
_____
☐ _____
_____
☐ _____
_____
☐ _____

"You can do it!"

Name something you didn't understand during your lesson today.

_____

_____

What can you do to figure it out?

_____

_____

HORSE INFORMATION RECORD

HORSE NAME _____

BARN NAME————————————BREED ——————

DATE OF BIRTH _____SEX _____

COLOR _____ HEIGHT_____

REGISTRATION # _____TATTOO _____

WHERE STABLED _____

PHONE NUMBER _____ *EMAIL* _____

VETERINARIAN_____

PHONE NUMBER _____ *EMAIL* _____

FARRIER_____

PHONE NUMBER _____ *EMAIL* _____

TRAINER_____

PHONE NUMBER _____ *EMAIL* _____

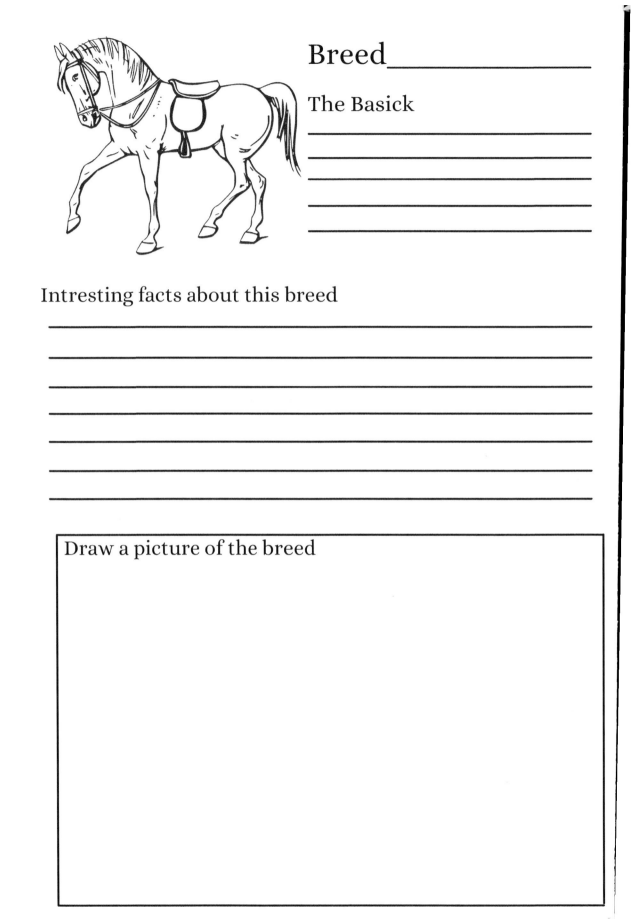

Breed_____

The Basick

_____
_____
_____
_____
_____

Intresting facts about this breed

_____
_____
_____
_____
_____
_____
_____

Draw a picture of the breed

Riding Lesson Journal

Date_____

_____

_____

Describe your Lesson:_____

_____

_____

Name 3 things that you learned today

1._____

_____

2._____

_____

3._____

_____

Need to improve

☐ ———————
☐ ———————
☐ ———————
☐ ———————
☐ ———————
☐ ———————
☐ ———————
☐ ———————
☐ ———————
☐ ———————

"You can do it!"

Name something you didn't understand during your lesson today.

_____

_____

What can you do to figure it out?

_____

_____

HORSE INFORMATION RECORD

HORSE NAME _____

BARN NAME _____ BREED _____

DATE OF BIRTH _____ SEX _____

COLOR _____ HEIGHT _____

REGISTRATION # _____ TATTOO _____

WHERE STABLED _____

PHONE NUMBER _____ *EMAIL* _____

VETERINARIAN _____

PHONE NUMBER _____ *EMAIL* _____

FARRIER _____

PHONE NUMBER _____ *EMAIL* _____

TRAINER _____

PHONE NUMBER _____ *EMAIL* _____

Breed_____

The Basick

_____
_____
_____
_____
_____

Intresting facts about this breed

_____
_____
_____
_____
_____
_____
_____

Draw a picture of the breed

Riding Lesson Journal

Date_____

_____

_____

Describe your Lesson:_____

_____

Name 3 things that you learned today

1._____

_____

2._____

_____

3._____

_____

Name something you didn't understand during your lesson today.

_____

_____

What can you do to figure it out?

_____

_____

Need to improve

☐ _____
☐ _____
☐ _____
☐ _____
☐ _____
☐ _____
☐ _____
☐ _____
☐ _____
☐ _____

"You can do it!"

HORSE INFORMATION RECORD

HORSE NAME _____

BARN NAME ———————————— BREED —————

DATE OF BIRTH _____ SEX _____

COLOR _____ HEIGHT _____

REGISTRATION # _____ TATTOO _____

WHERE STABLED _____

PHONE NUMBER _____ *EMAIL* _____

VETERINARIAN _____

PHONE NUMBER _____ *EMAIL* _____

FARRIER _____

PHONE NUMBER _____ *EMAIL* _____

TRAINER _____

PHONE NUMBER _____ *EMAIL* _____

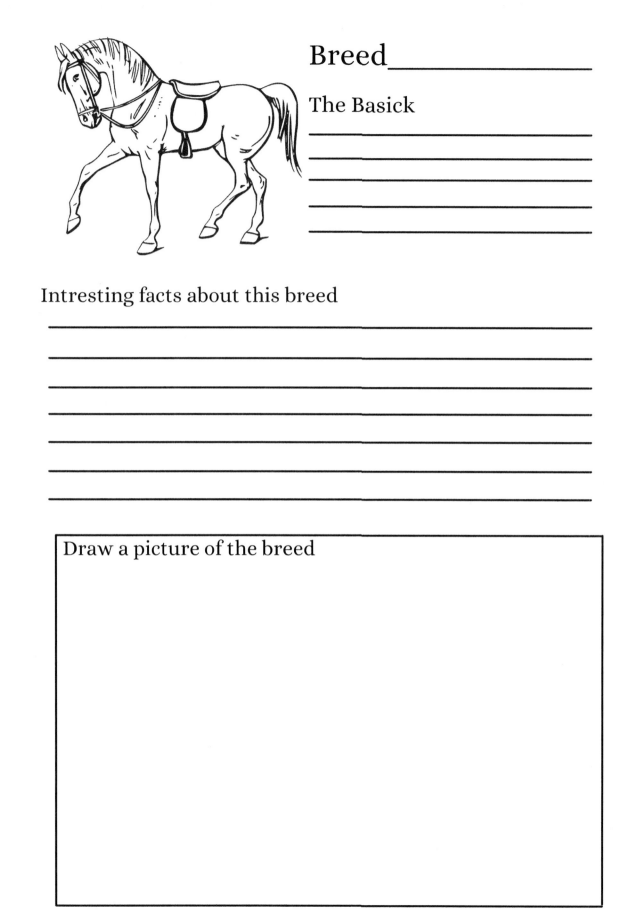

Breed_____

The Basick

_____
_____
_____
_____
_____

Intresting facts about this breed

_____
_____
_____
_____
_____
_____
_____
_____

Draw a picture of the breed

Riding Lesson Journal

Date_____

☐ ——————
☐ ——————
☐ ——————
☐ ——————
☐ ——————
☐ ——————
☐ ——————
☐ ——————
☐ ——————
☐ ——————

_____

_____

Describe your Lesson:_____

_____

_____

Name 3 things that you learned today

1._____

_____

2._____

_____

3._____

_____

"You can do it!"

Name something you didn't understand during your lesson today.

_____

_____

What can you do to figure it out?

_____

_____

HORSE INFORMATION RECORD

HORSE NAME _____

BARN NAME _____ BREED _____

DATE OF BIRTH _____ SEX _____

COLOR _____ HEIGHT _____

REGISTRATION # _____ TATTOO _____

WHERE STABLED _____

PHONE NUMBER _____ *EMAIL* _____

VETERINARIAN _____

PHONE NUMBER _____ *EMAIL* _____

FARRIER _____

PHONE NUMBER _____ *EMAIL* _____

TRAINER _____

PHONE NUMBER _____ *EMAIL* _____

Breed_____

The Basick

_____
_____
_____
_____
_____

Intresting facts about this breed

_____
_____
_____
_____
_____
_____
_____

Draw a picture of the breed

Riding Lesson Journal

Date_____

_____

_____

Describe your Lesson:_____

_____

_____

Name 3 things that you learned today

1._____

_____

2. _____

_____

3. _____

_____

Name something you didn't understand during your lesson today.

_____

_____

What can you do to figure it out?

_____

_____

Need to improve

☐ _____
☐ _____
☐ _____
☐ _____
☐ _____
☐ _____
☐ _____
☐ _____
☐ _____
☐ _____

"You can do it!"

HORSE INFORMATION RECORD

HORSE NAME _____

BARN NAME —————————— BREED —————

DATE OF BIRTH _____ SEX _____

COLOR _____ HEIGHT _____

REGISTRATION # _____ TATTOO _____

WHERE STABLED _____

PHONE NUMBER _____ *EMAIL* _____

VETERINARIAN _____

PHONE NUMBER _____ *EMAIL* _____

FARRIER _____

PHONE NUMBER _____ *EMAIL* _____

TRAINER _____

PHONE NUMBER _____ *EMAIL* _____

Breed_____

The Basick

_____
_____
_____
_____
_____

Intresting facts about this breed

_____
_____
_____
_____
_____
_____
_____
_____

Draw a picture of the breed

Riding Lesson Journal

Date_____

_____

_____

Describe your Lesson:_____

_____

_____

Name 3 things that you learned today

1._____

_____

2._____

_____

3._____

_____

Name something you didn't understand during your lesson today.

_____

_____

What can you do to figure it out?

_____

_____

Need to improve

☐ _____
☐ _____
☐ _____
☐ _____
☐ _____
☐ _____
☐ _____
☐ _____
☐ _____
☐ _____

"You can do it!"

HORSE INFORMATION RECORD

HORSE NAME _____

BARN NAME——————————BREED _____

DATE OF BIRTH_____SEX _____

COLOR _____ HEIGHT_____

REGISTRATION # _____TATTOO _____

WHERE STABLED _____

PHONE NUMBER _____ *EMAIL* _____

VETERINARIAN_____

PHONE NUMBER _____ *EMAIL* _____

FARRIER _____

PHONE NUMBER _____ *EMAIL* _____

TRAINER _____

PHONE NUMBER _____ *EMAIL* _____

Breed_____

The Basick

_____
_____
_____
_____
_____

Intresting facts about this breed

_____
_____
_____
_____
_____
_____
_____

Draw a picture of the breed

Riding Lesson Journal

Date_____

_____

_____

Describe your Lesson:_____

_____

_____

Name 3 things that you learned today

1._____

_____

2. _____

_____

3. _____

_____

Name something you didn't understand during your lesson today.

_____

_____

What can you do to figure it out?

_____

_____

HORSE INFORMATION RECORD

HORSE NAME _____

BARN NAME ————————————— BREED _____

DATE OF BIRTH _____ SEX _____

COLOR _____ HEIGHT _____

REGISTRATION # _____ TATTOO _____

WHERE STABLED _____

PHONE NUMBER _____ *EMAIL* _____

VETERINARIAN _____

PHONE NUMBER _____ *EMAIL* _____

FARRIER _____

PHONE NUMBER _____ *EMAIL* _____

TRAINER _____

PHONE NUMBER _____ *EMAIL* _____

Breed_____

The Basick

_____
_____
_____
_____
_____

Intresting facts about this breed

_____
_____
_____
_____
_____
_____
_____
_____

Draw a picture of the breed

Riding Lesson Journal

Date_____

_____

_____

Describe your Lesson:_____

_____

_____

Name 3 things that you learned today

1._____

_____

2. _____

_____

3. _____

_____

Name something you didn't understand during your lesson today.

_____

_____

What can you do to figure it out?

_____

_____

Need to improve

☐ _____
☐ _____
☐ _____
☐ _____
☐ _____
☐ _____
☐ _____
☐ _____
☐ _____
☐ _____

"You can do it!"

HORSE INFORMATION RECORD

HORSE NAME _____

BARN NAME ——————— BREED _____

DATE OF BIRTH _____ SEX _____

COLOR _____ HEIGHT_____

REGISTRATION # _____ TATTOO _____

WHERE STABLED _____

PHONE NUMBER _____ *EMAIL* _____

VETERINARIAN _____

PHONE NUMBER _____ *EMAIL* _____

FARRIER _____

PHONE NUMBER _____ *EMAIL* _____

TRAINER _____

PHONE NUMBER _____ *EMAIL* _____

Breed_____

The Basick

_____
_____
_____
_____
_____

Intresting facts about this breed

_____
_____
_____
_____
_____
_____
_____

Draw a picture of the breed

Riding Lesson Journal

Date _____

_____

_____

Describe your Lesson:_____

_____

_____

Name 3 things that you learned today

1._____

_____

2._____

_____

3._____

_____

Name something you didn't understand during your lesson today.

_____

_____

What can you do to figure it out?

_____

_____

Need to improve

☐ _____
  _____
☐ _____
  _____
☐ _____
  _____
☐ _____
☐ _____
☐ _____
☐ _____
☐ _____
☐ _____

"You can do it!"